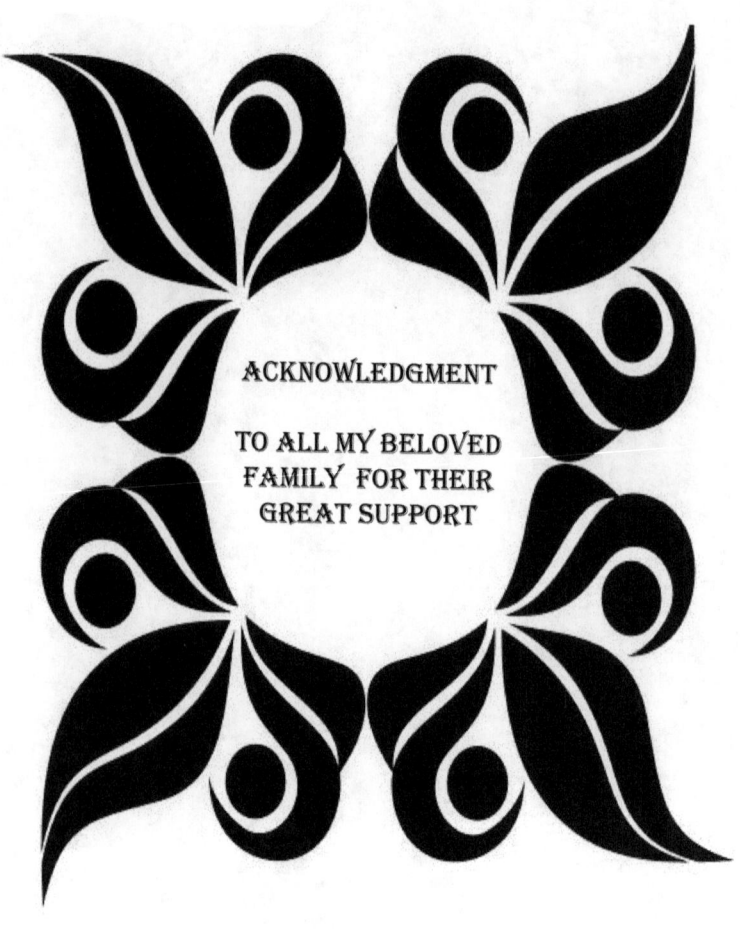

ACKNOWLEDGMENT

TO ALL MY BELOVED
FAMILY FOR THEIR
GREAT SUPPORT

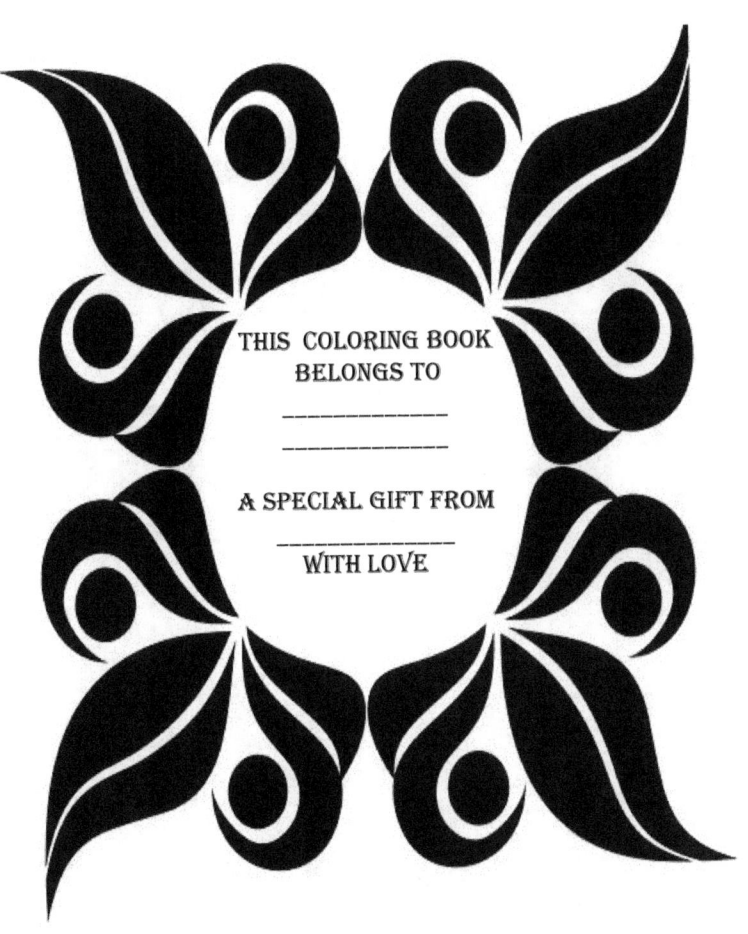

THIS COLORING BOOK
BELONGS TO

_____
_____

A SPECIAL GIFT FROM
_____
WITH LOVE

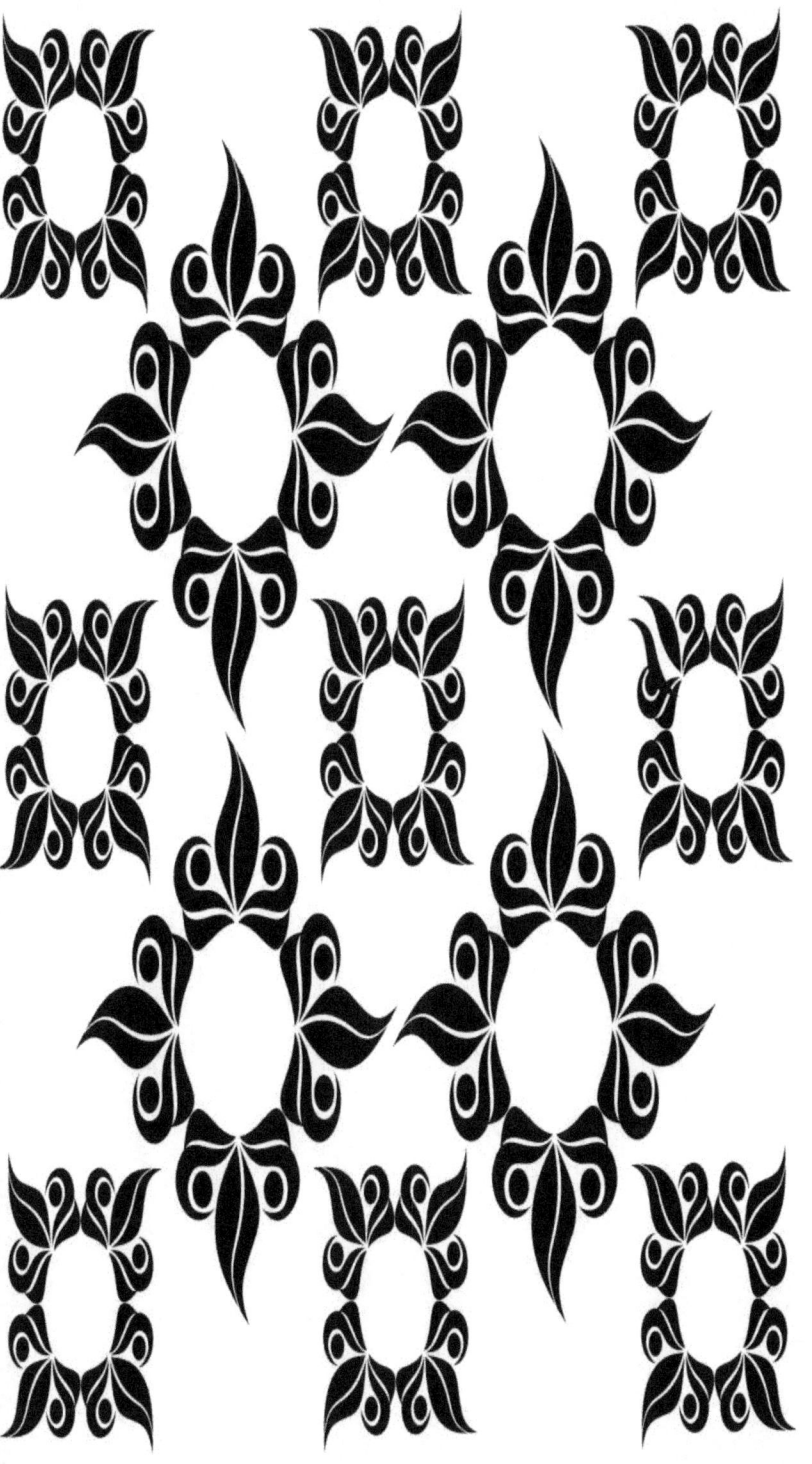

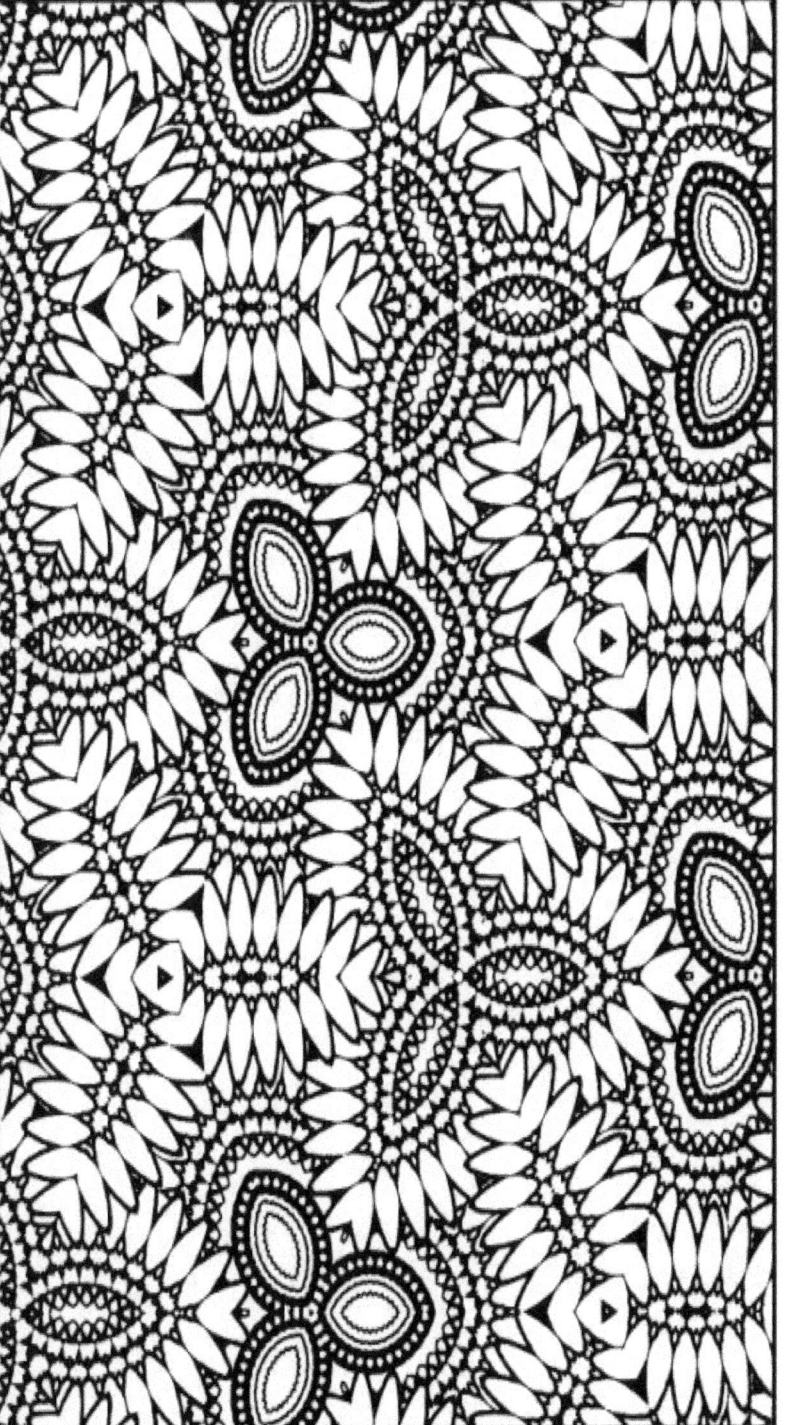

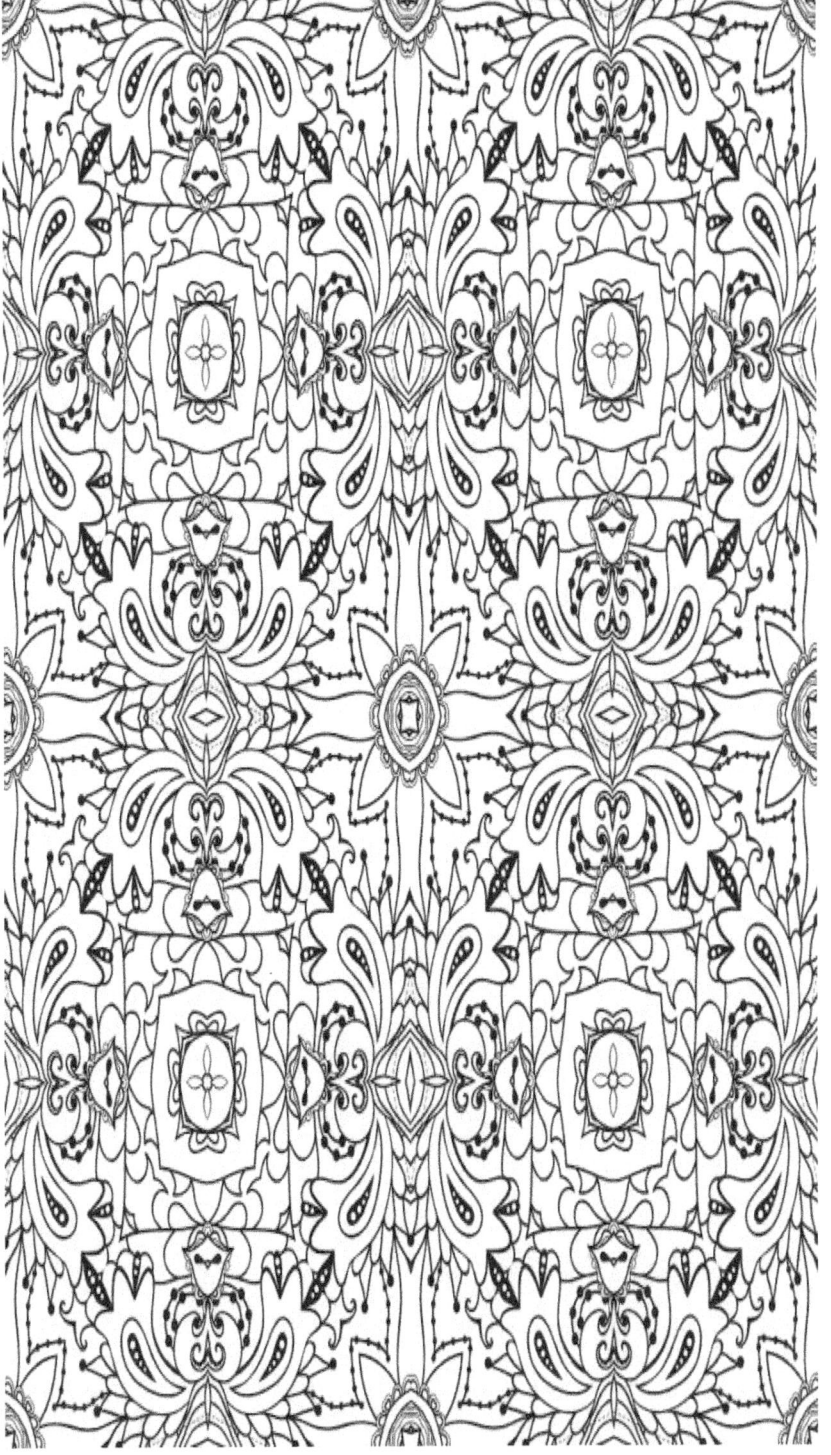

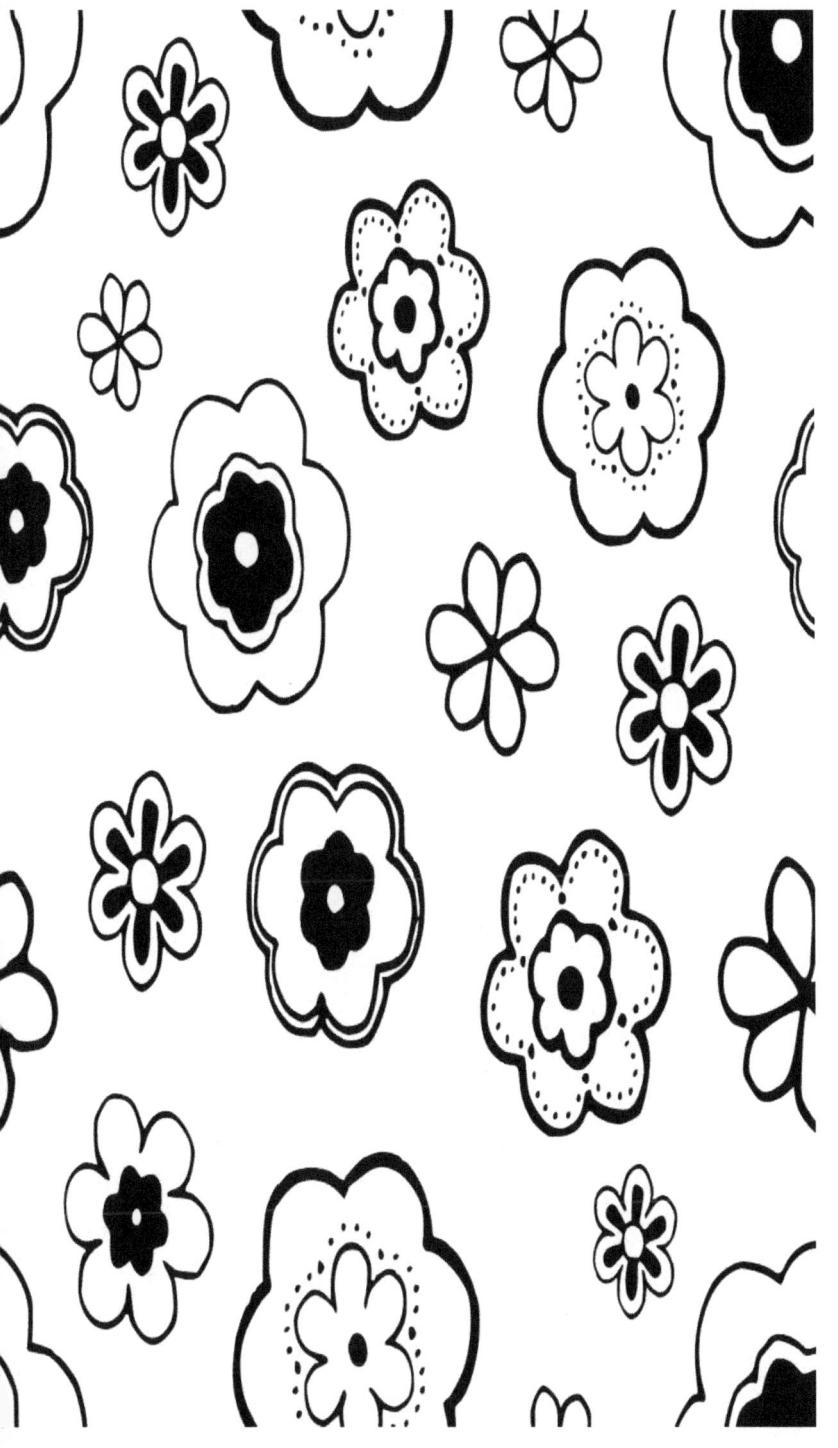

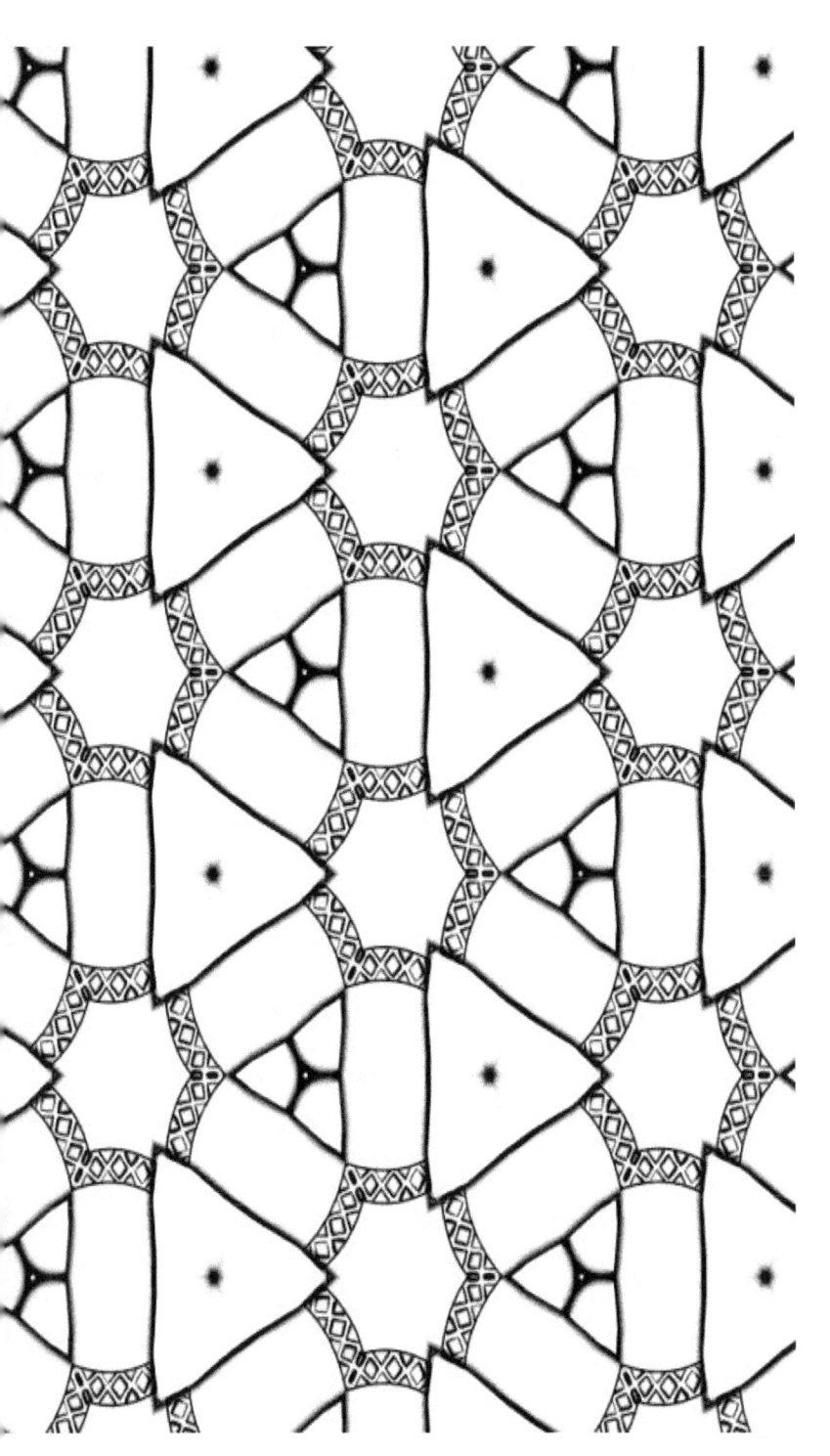

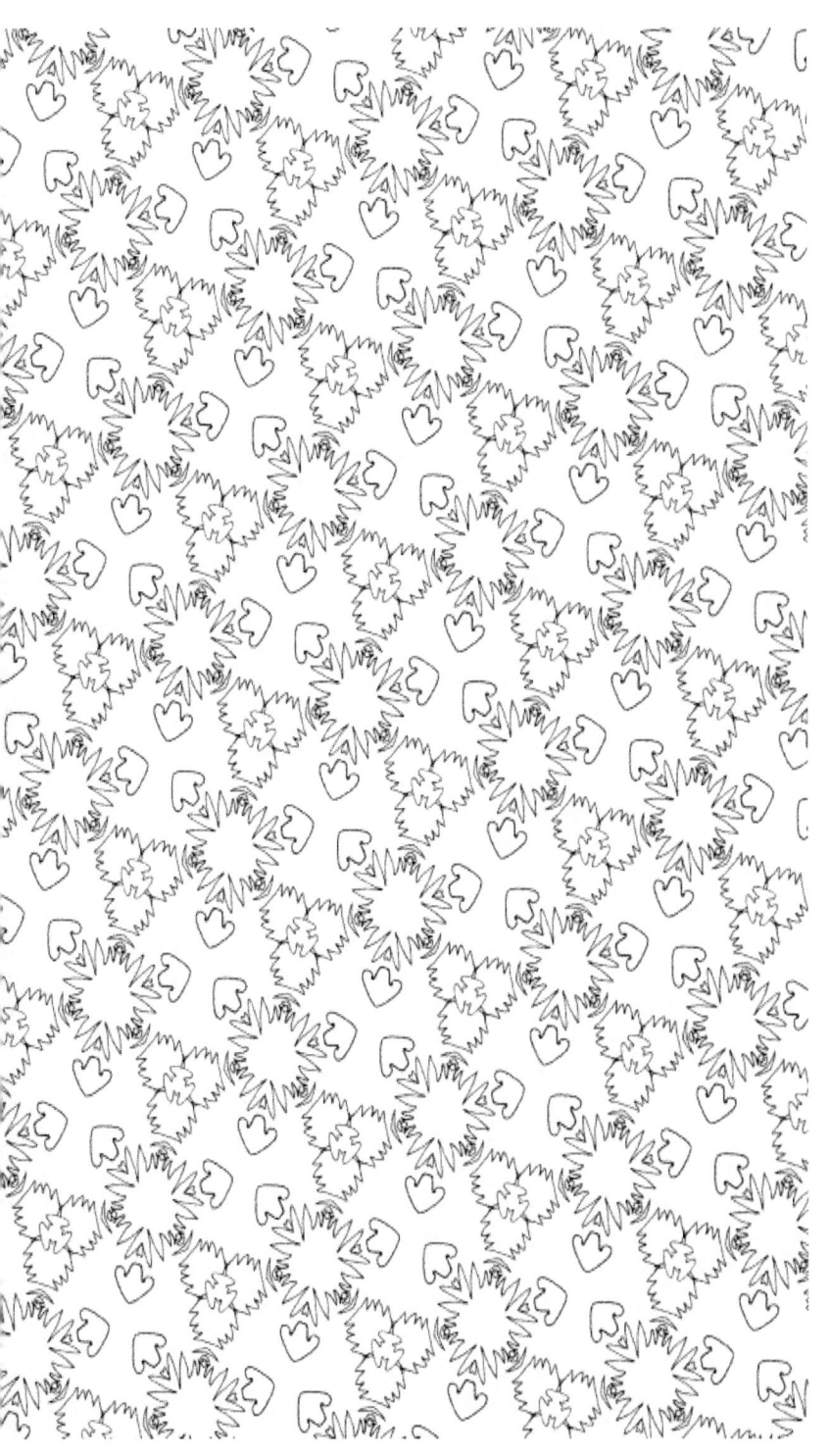

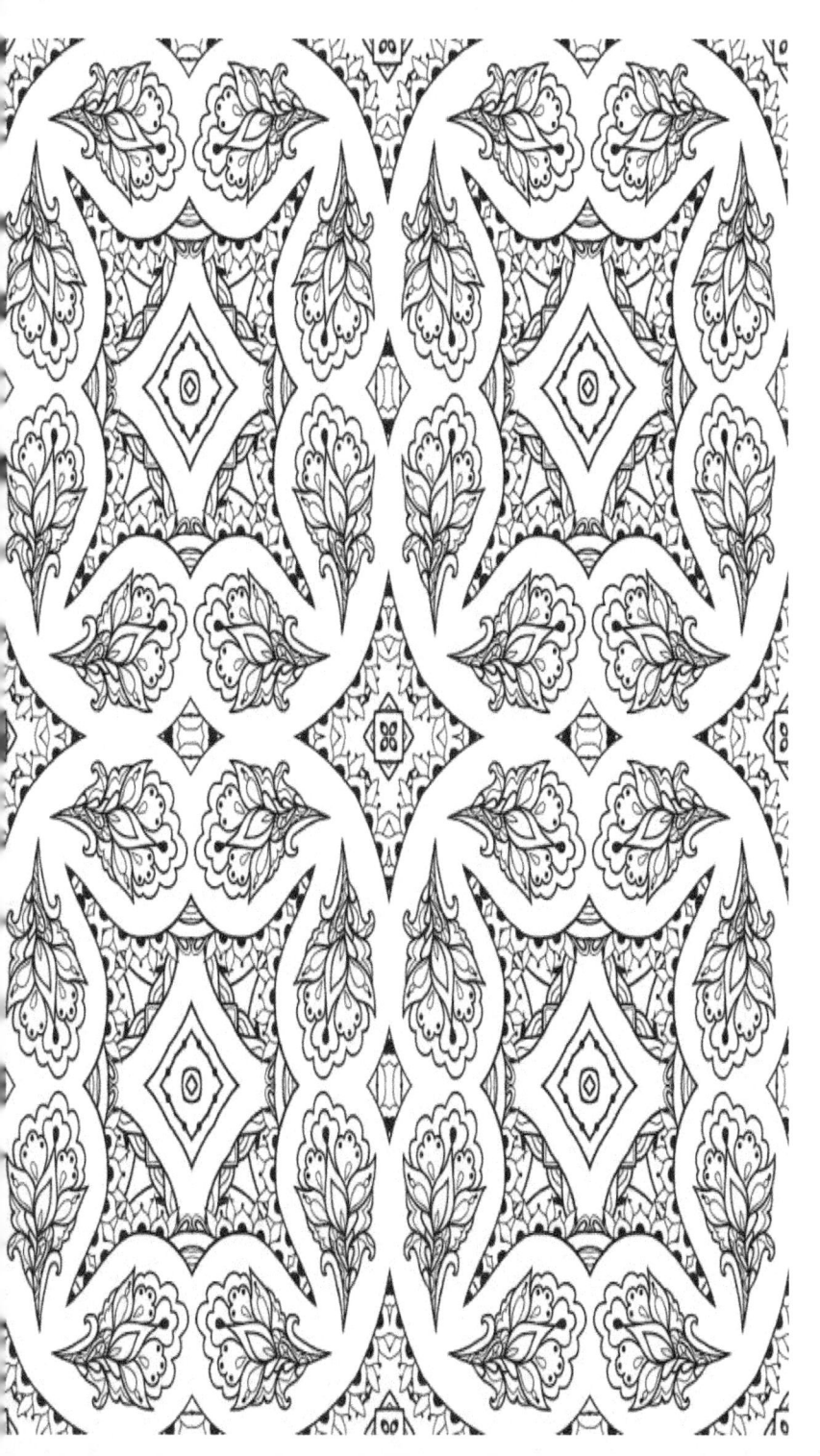

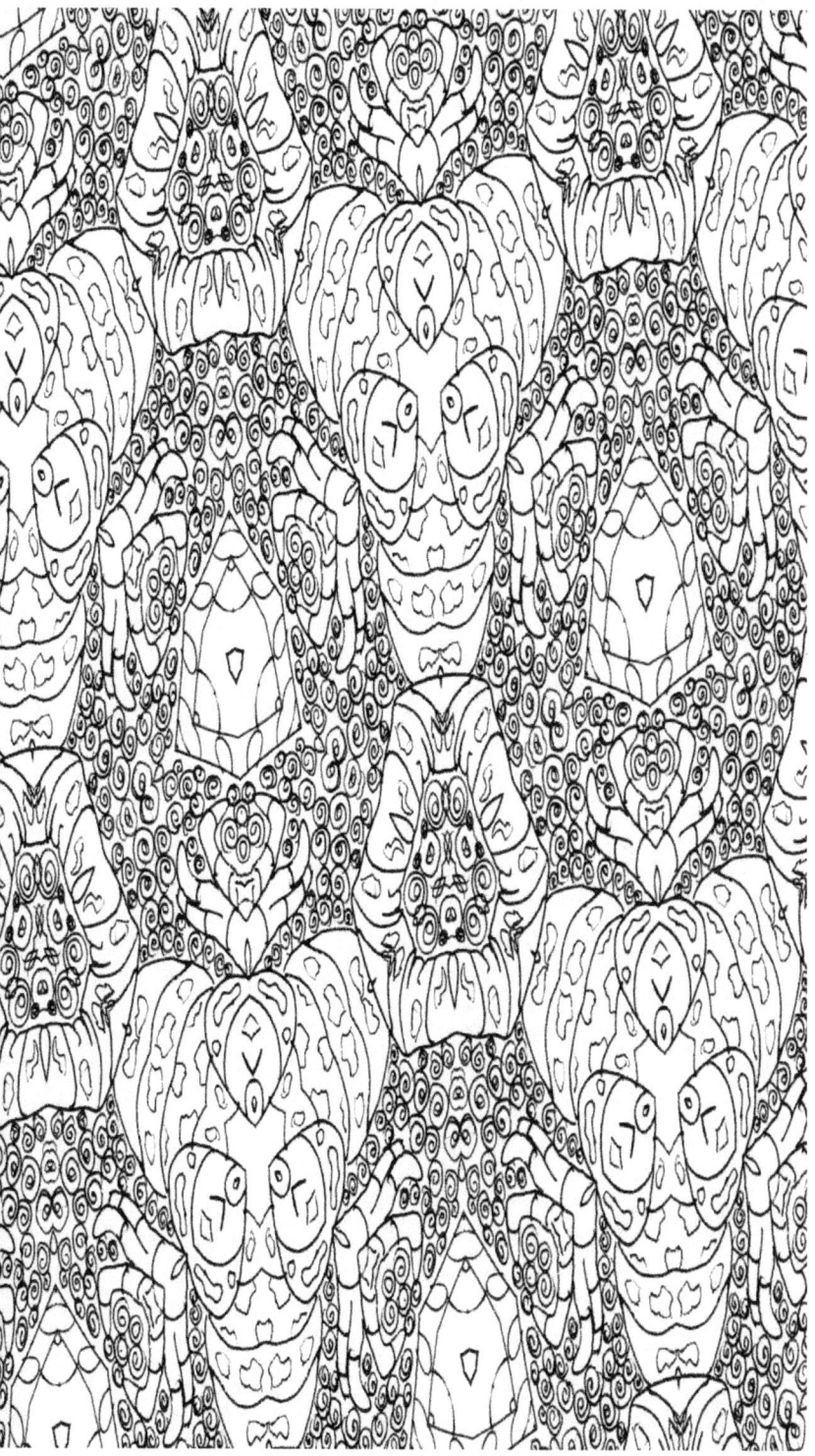

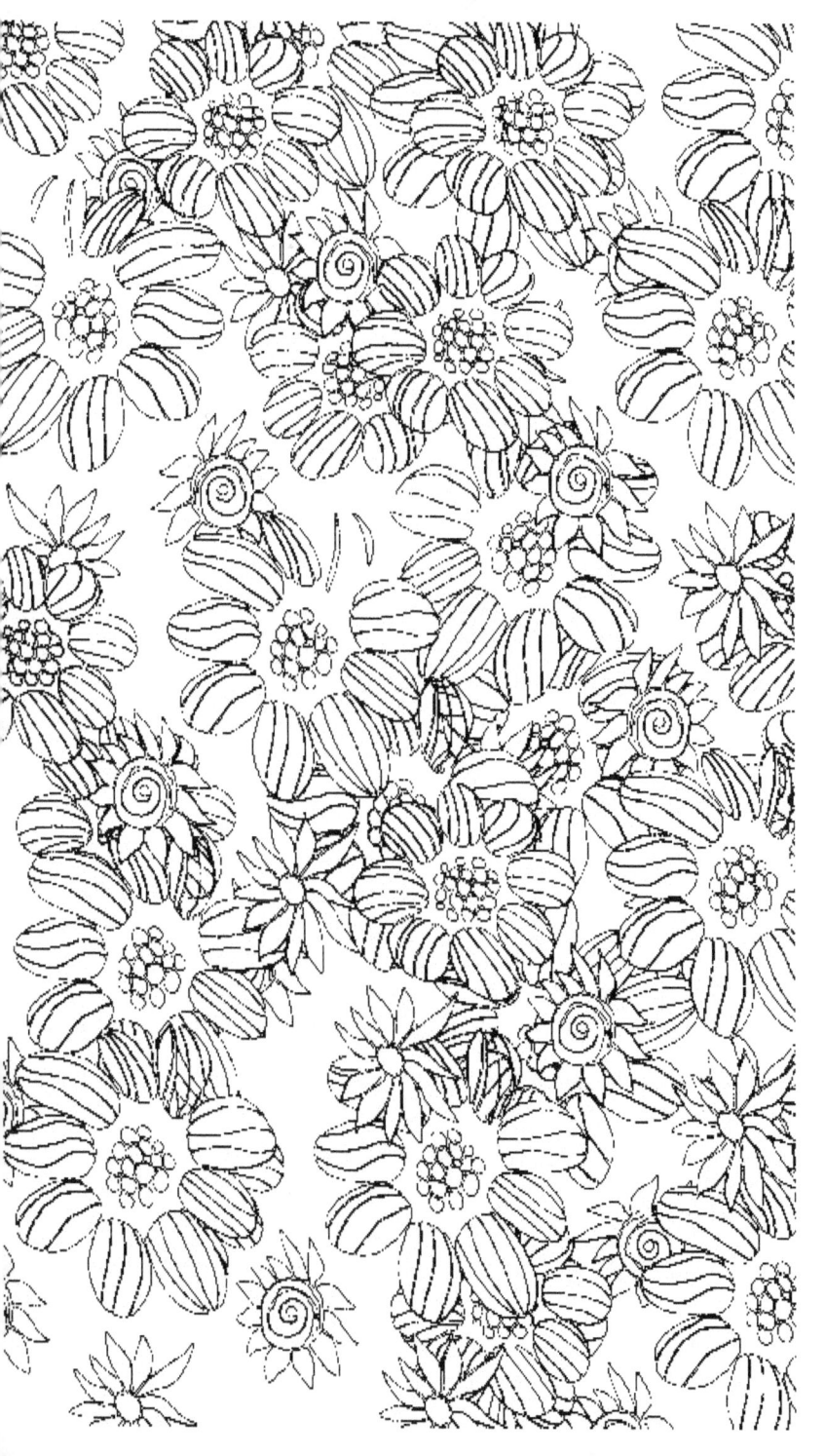

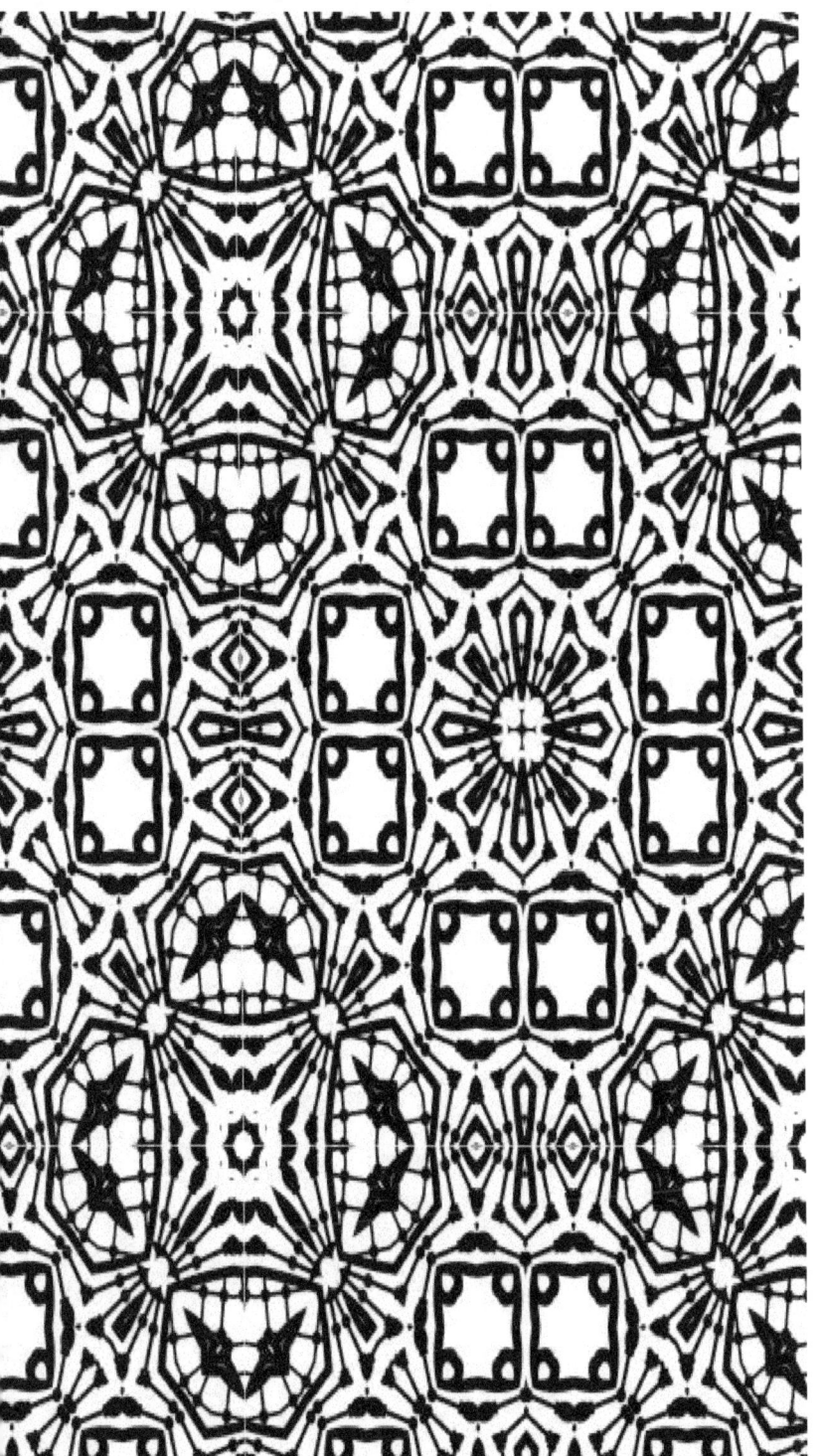

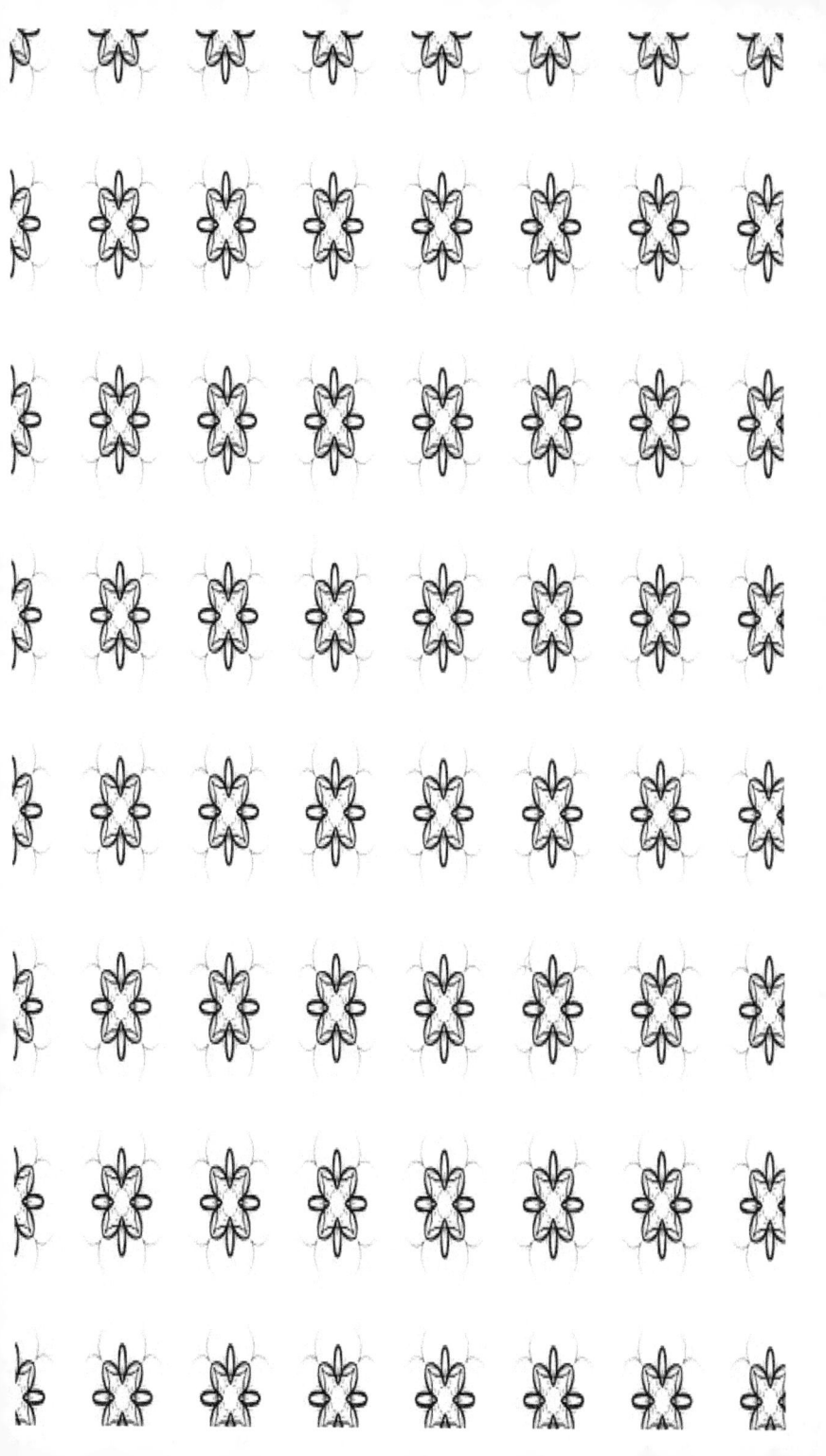

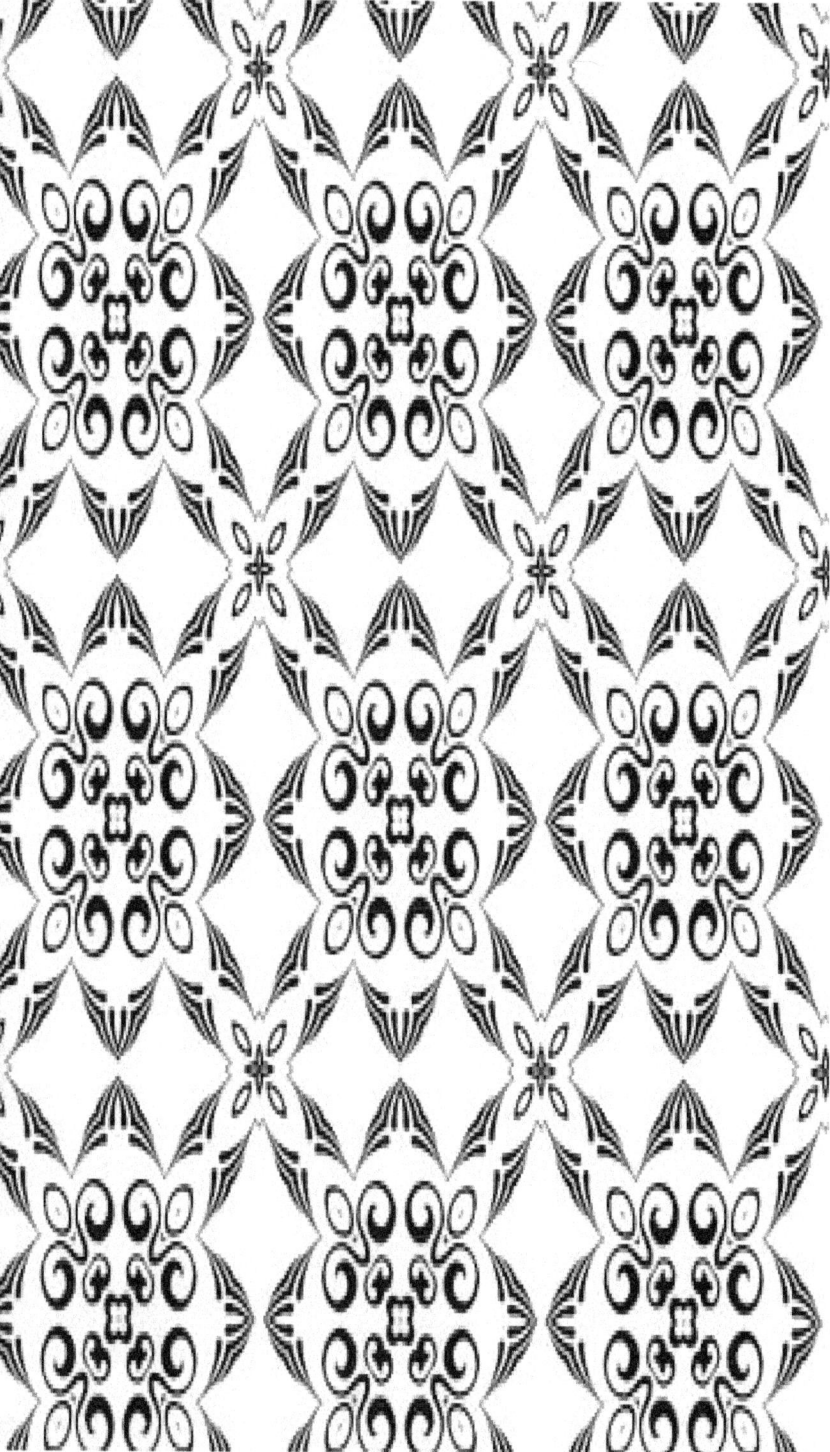

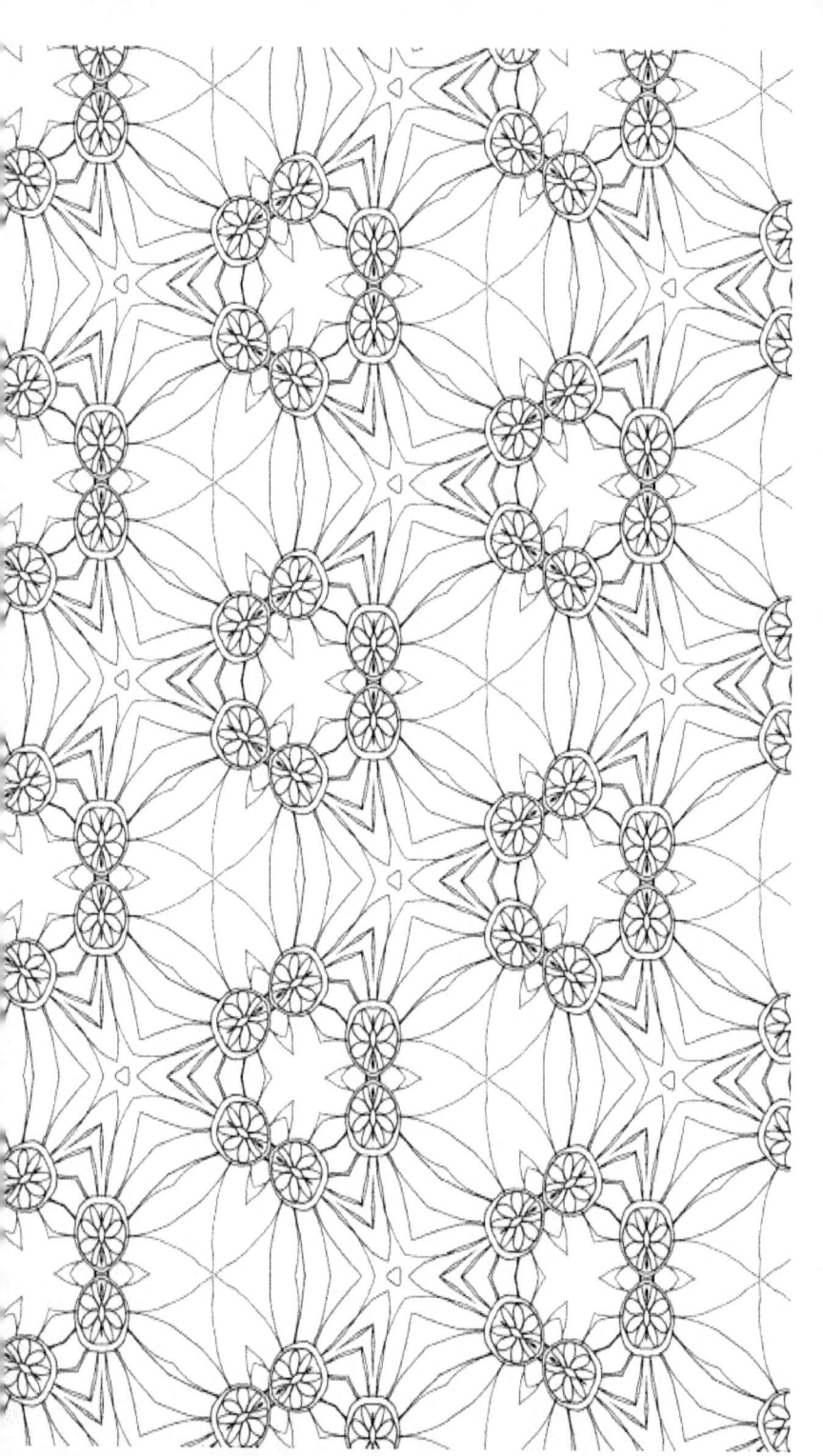

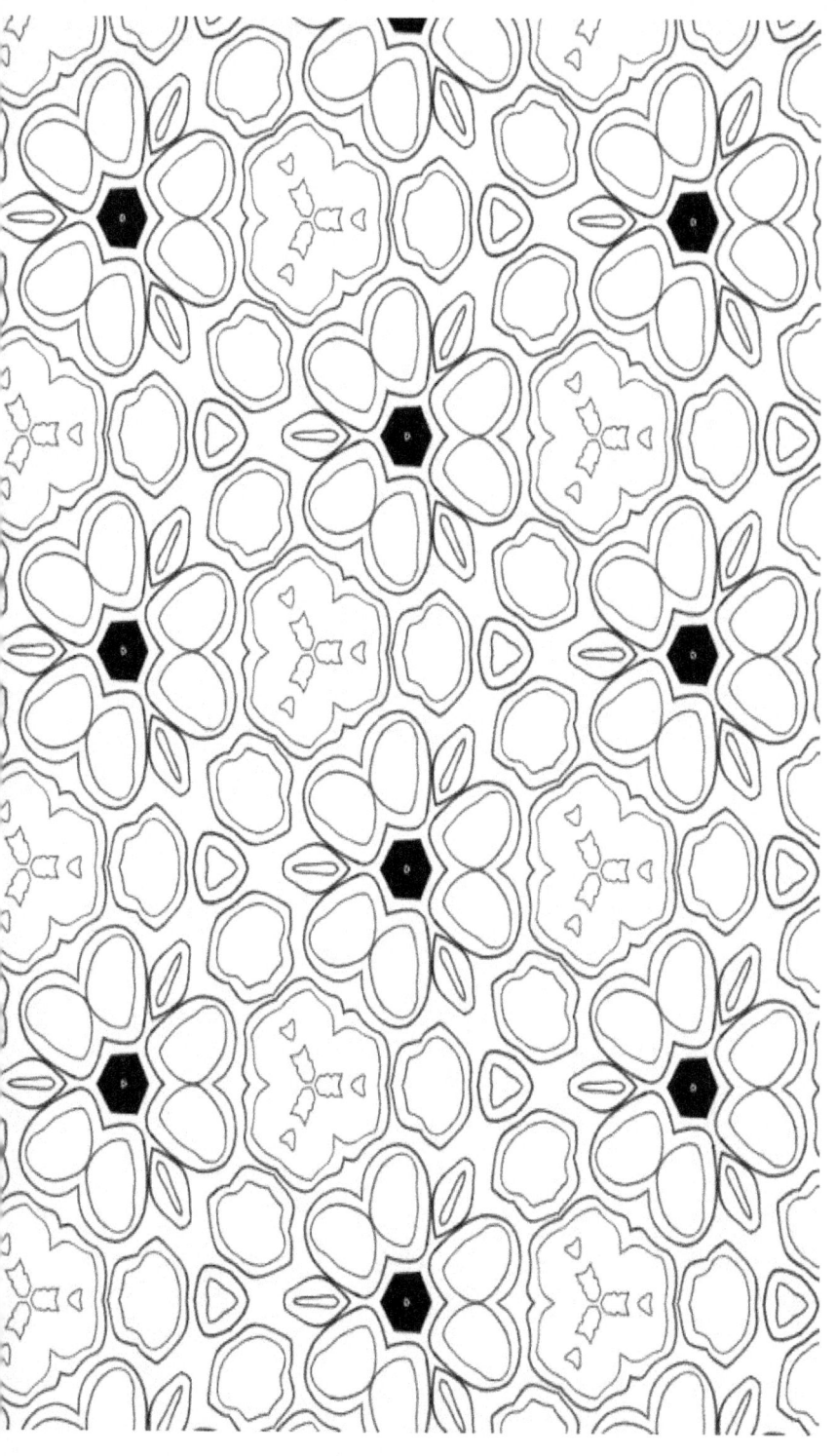

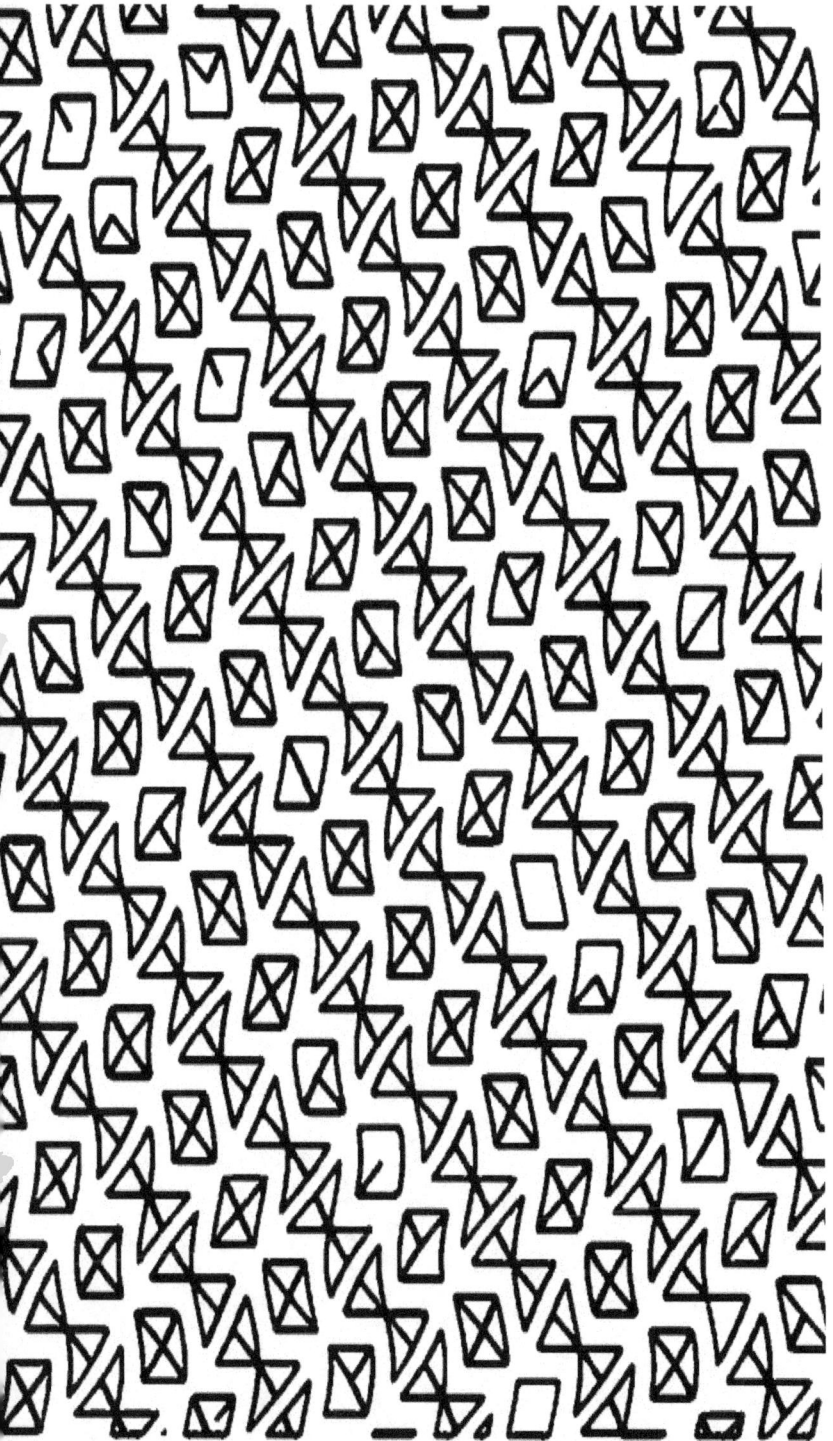

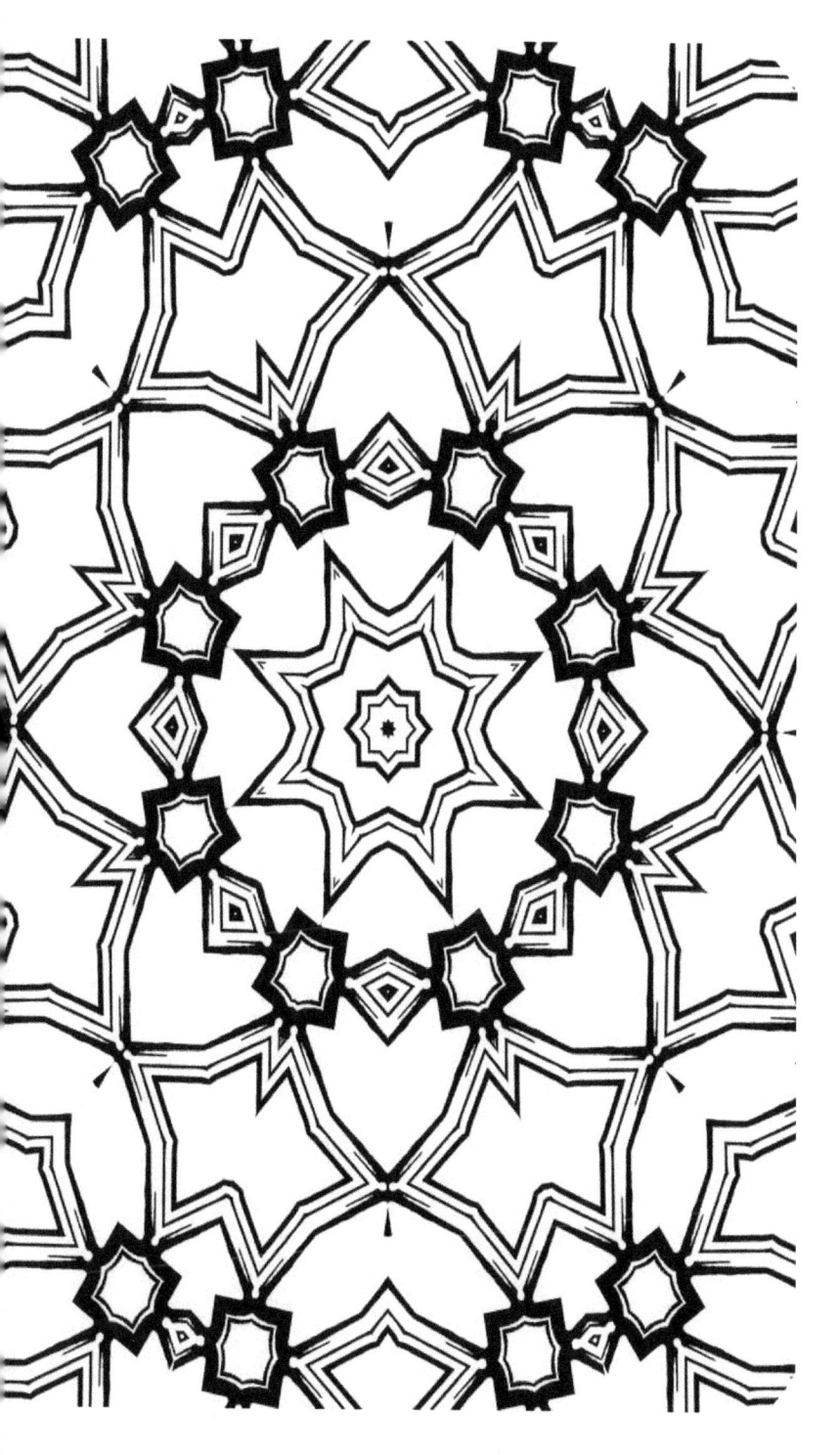

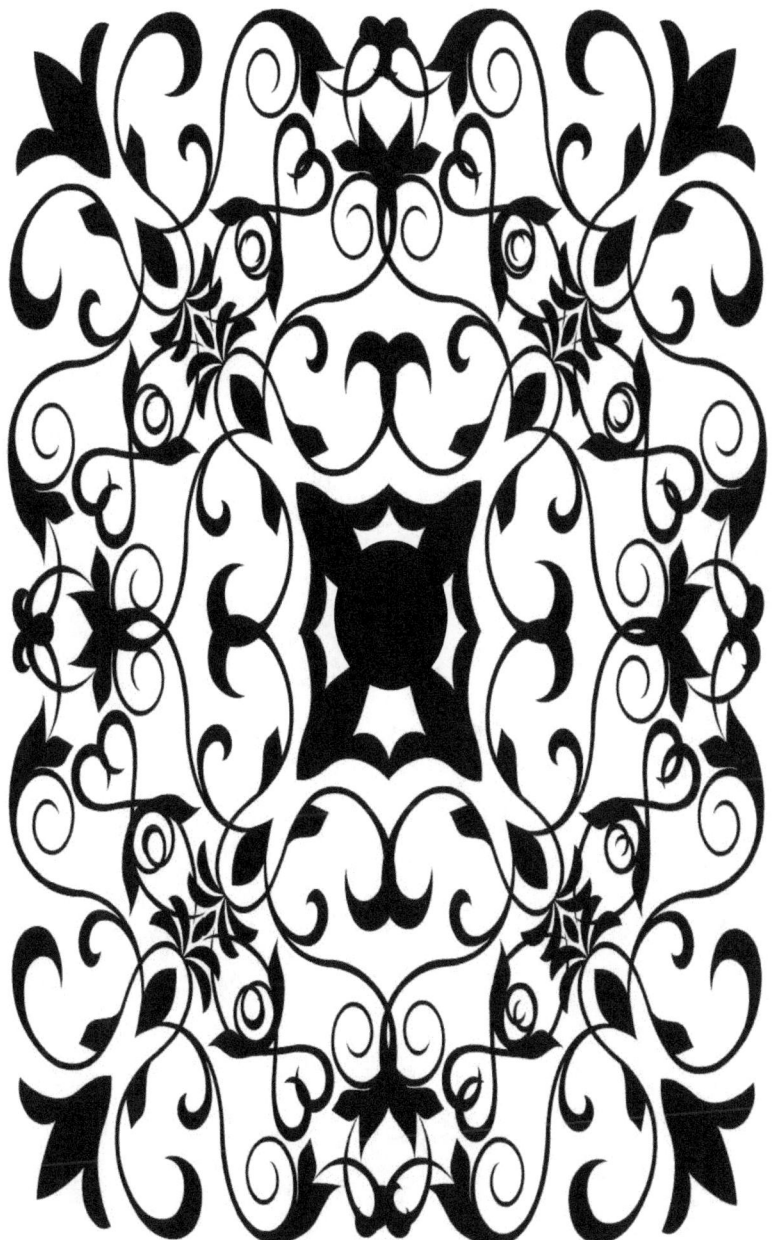

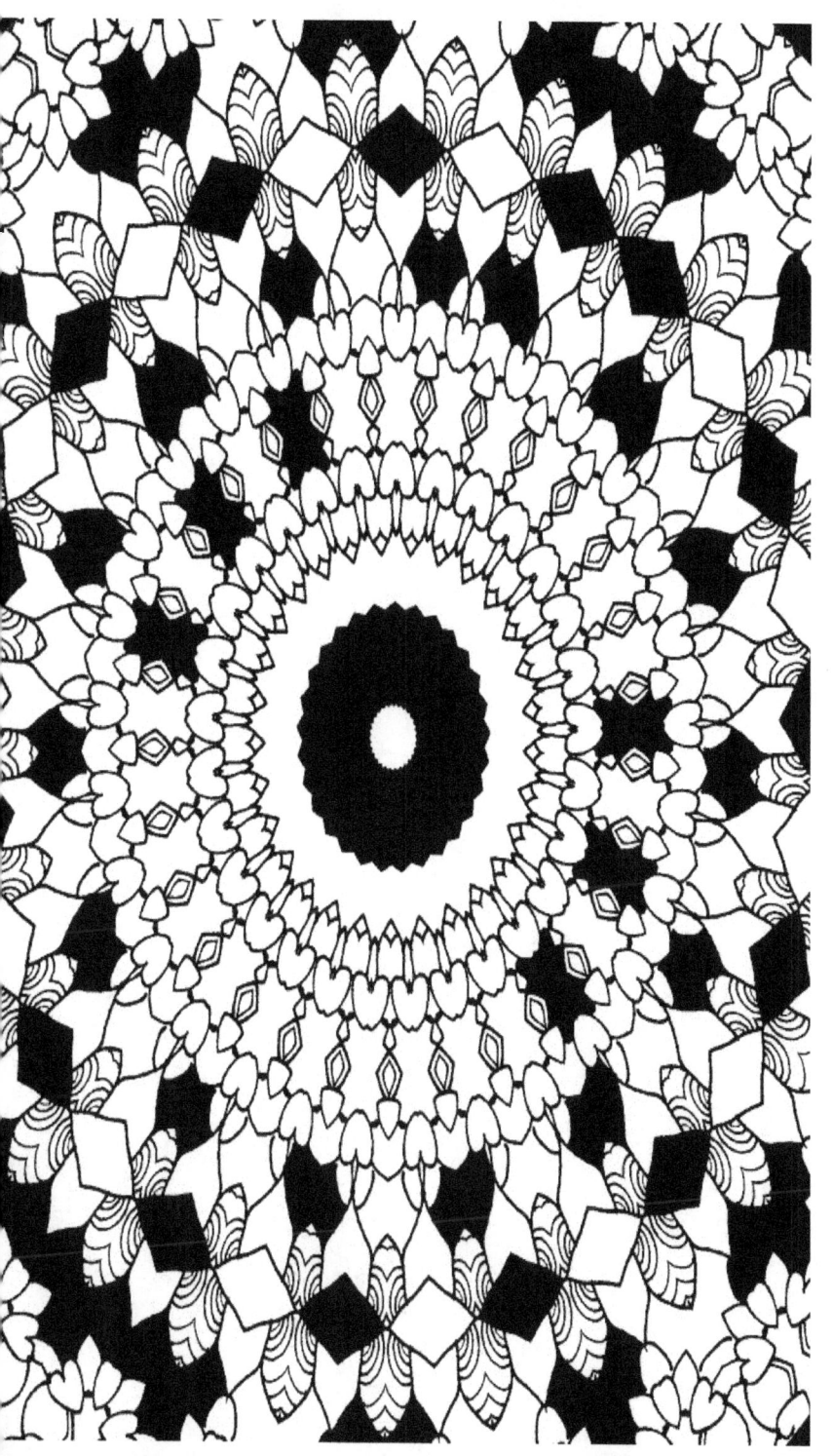

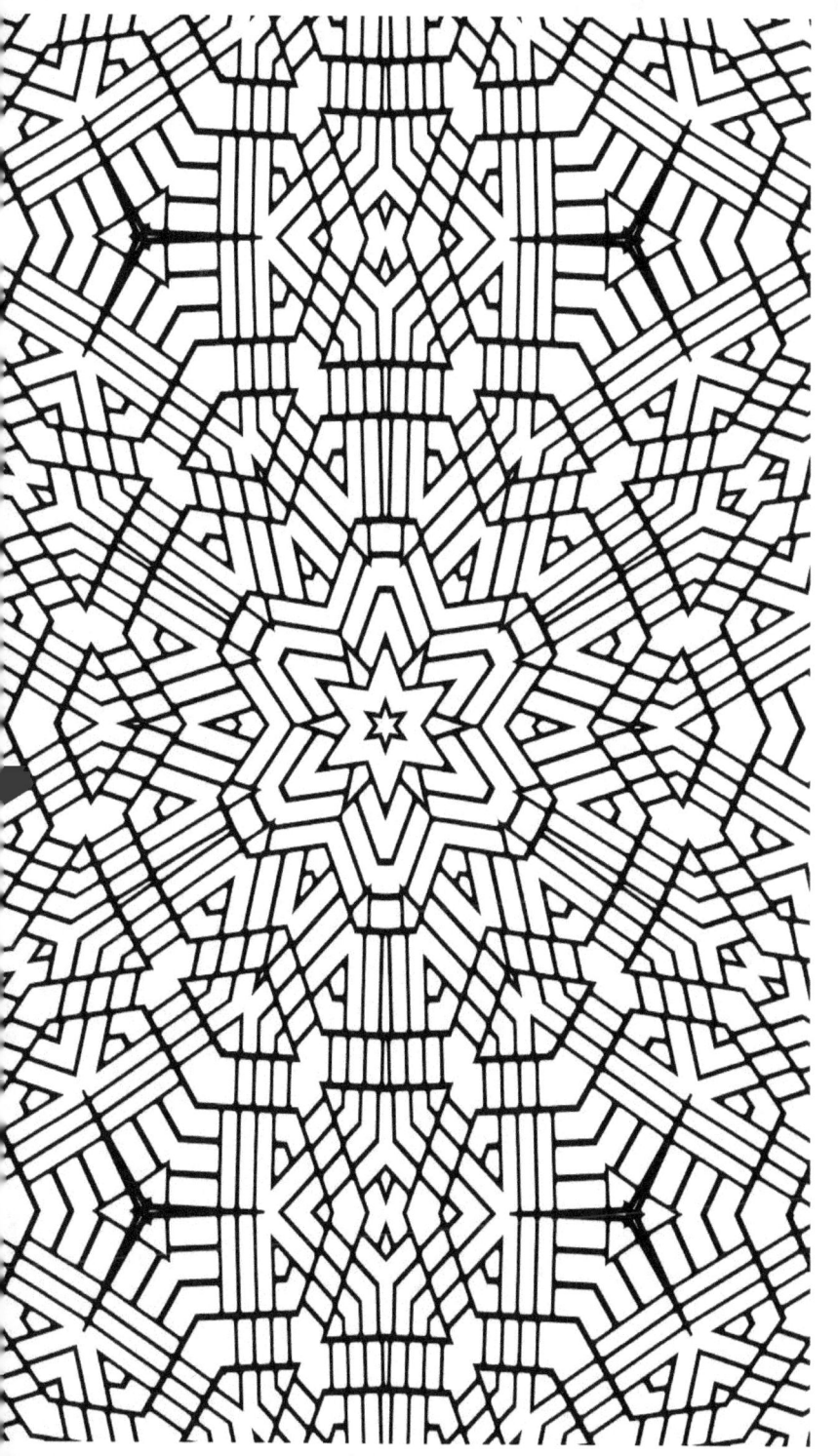

Color Testing Page

www.ingramcontent.com/pod-product-compliance
Lightning Source LLC
Chambersburg PA
CBHW051823170526
45167CB00005B/2139